WHAT IS A FRUIT?

What is a FRUIT?

by Jenifer W. Day

illustrated by Enid Kotschnig

 GOLDEN PRESS • NEW YORK

Western Publishing Company, Inc., Racine, Wisconsin

TABLE OF CONTENTS

This is a tomato.
A tomato is a fruit.
A tomato is a simple fleshy fruit.
It has a thin skin on the outside
and many seeds on the inside.
A tomato is the ripened ovary
of a single flower.

There are many simple, fleshy fruits.
Some of them are called vegetables.

sepals

seeds

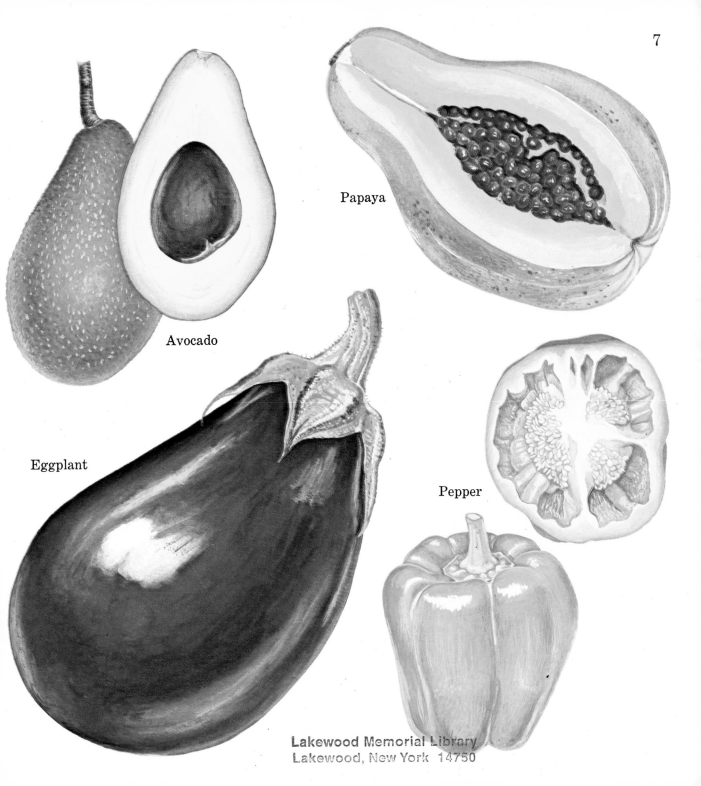

Papaya

Avocado

Eggplant

Pepper

8

This is a watermelon.
A watermelon is a fruit.
A watermelon is a simple fleshy fruit.
It has a hard rind on the outside
and many seeds on the inside.
A watermelon is the ripened ovary
of a single flower.

There are many kinds of simple fleshy fruits.

Pumpkin

Gourd

Acorn Squash

Crooked Neck Squash

Turban Squash

Cantaloupe

Cucumber

pistil
stamens
ovary

This is an orange.
An orange is a citrus fruit.
It has a leathery skin on the outside
    and seeds on the inside.
An orange is the ripened ovary of a flower.

There are many kinds of citrus fruits.

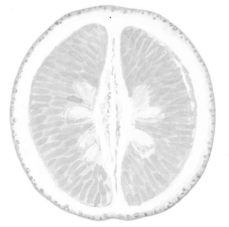

seeds

11

Kumquat

Lemon

Grapefruit

Tangerine

Lime

ovary

male flower

This is a banana.
A banana is a fruit.
A banana is a sweet fleshy fruit.
It has a tough skin on the outside
    and no seeds on the inside.
A banana is the ripened ovary of a flower.
Only the wild ones have seeds.

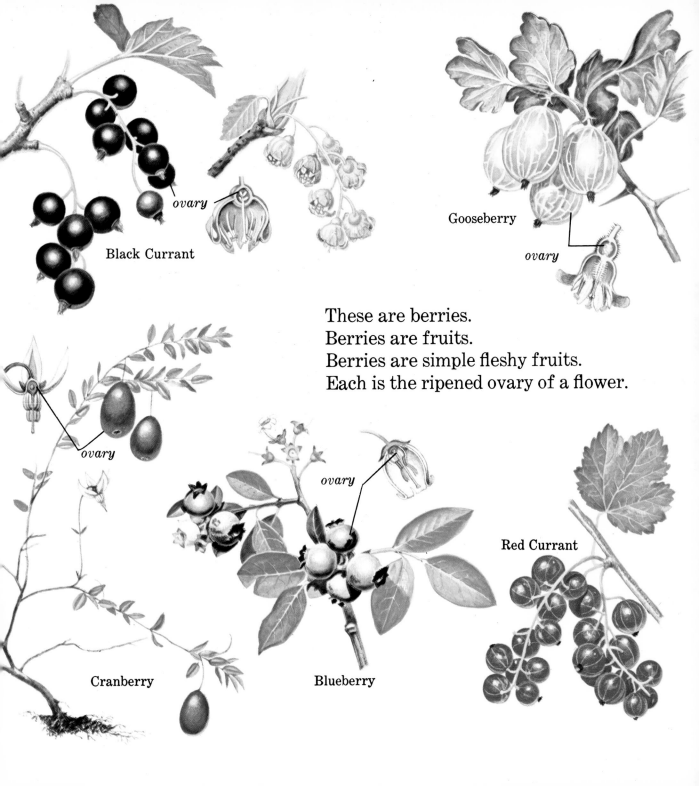

ovary

Black Currant

Gooseberry

ovary

ovary

These are berries.
Berries are fruits.
Berries are simple fleshy fruits.
Each is the ripened ovary of a flower.

ovary

Red Currant

Cranberry

Blueberry

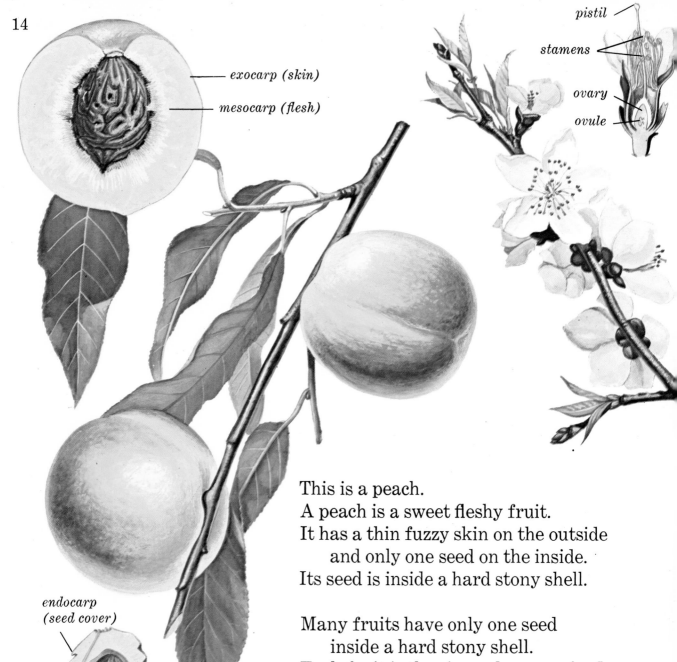

exocarp (skin)

mesocarp (flesh)

pistil

stamens

ovary

ovule

endocarp
(seed cover)

seed

This is a peach.
A peach is a sweet fleshy fruit.
It has a thin fuzzy skin on the outside
    and only one seed on the inside.
Its seed is inside a hard stony shell.

Many fruits have only one seed
    inside a hard stony shell.
Each fruit is the ripened ovary of a flower.

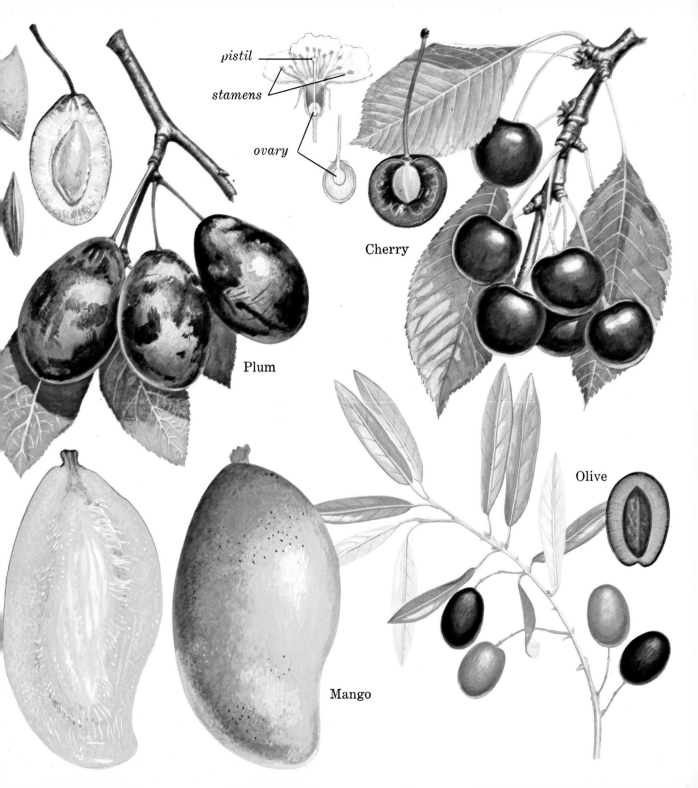

pistil

stamens

ovary

Cherry

Plum

Mango

Olive

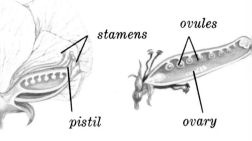

stamens

ovules

pistil

ovary

flower

These are green peas.
Green peas are fruits.
Green peas are dry fruits
   with a pod on the outside,
   and seeds on the inside.
A green pea is the ripened ovary
   of a flower.
The seeds develop from the ovules.
Plants that have seed pods
   are called legumes.

mature ovary (fruit)

seeds

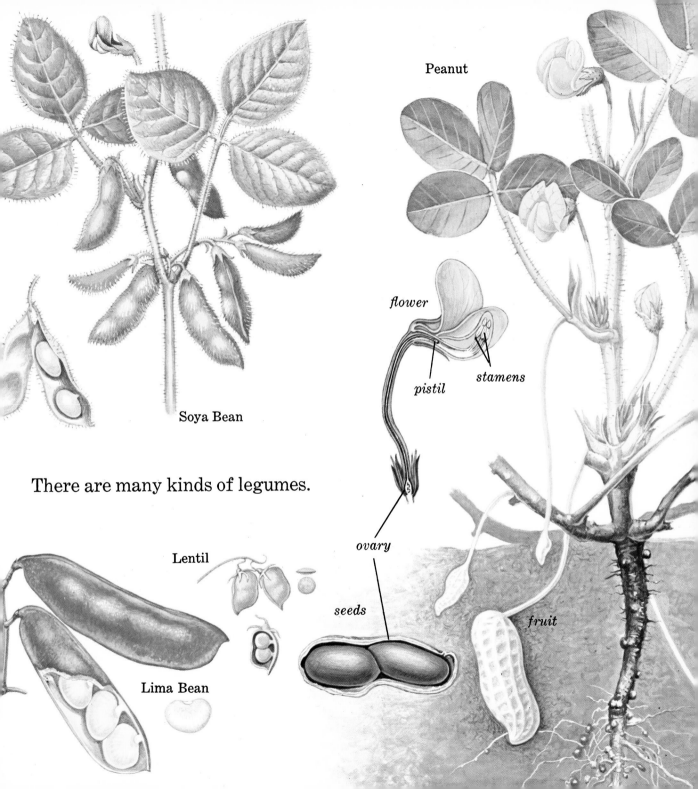

Peanut

Soya Bean

flower

pistil

stamens

There are many kinds of legumes.

Lentil

ovary

seeds

Lima Bean

fruit

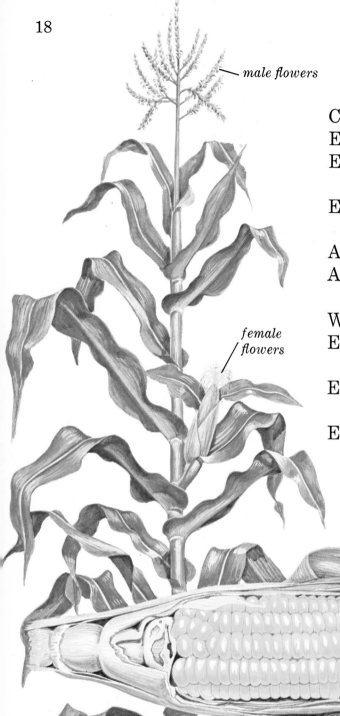

male flowers

pollen

female flowers

Corn is a grain.
Each grain of corn is a fruit.
Each grain of corn is a dry fruit
    with a single seed.
Each grain of corn is the ripened
    ovary of a flower.
An ear of corn has many flowers.
An ear of corn has many grains.

Wheat and rice are grains.
Each grain is a dry fruit with
    a single seed.
Each grain is the ripened ovary
    of a flower.
Each flowering stalk
    has many flowers.

corn silks
(pistils)

many female
flowers on ear

fruit

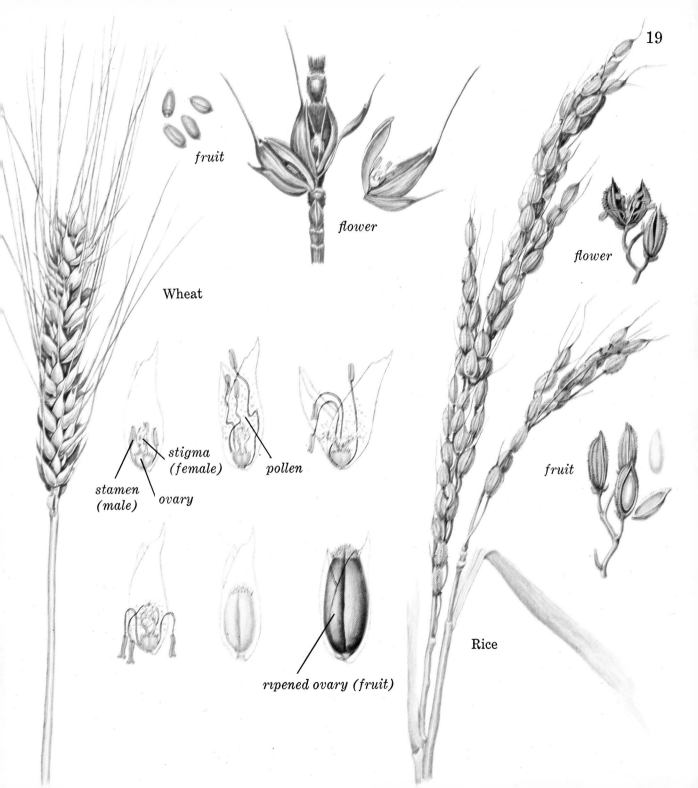

19

fruit

flower

Wheat

flower

stigma (female)

pollen

stamen (male)

ovary

fruit

Rice

ripened ovary (fruit)

pollen

female flower

male flower

ovary

This is a walnut.
A walnut is a fruit.
A walnut is a dry fruit.
It has a thick skin on the outside
    and only one seed on the inside.
The seed is inside a hard shell.
The seed is the part we eat.
A walnut is the ripened ovary of a flower.

fruit

skin

shell

seed

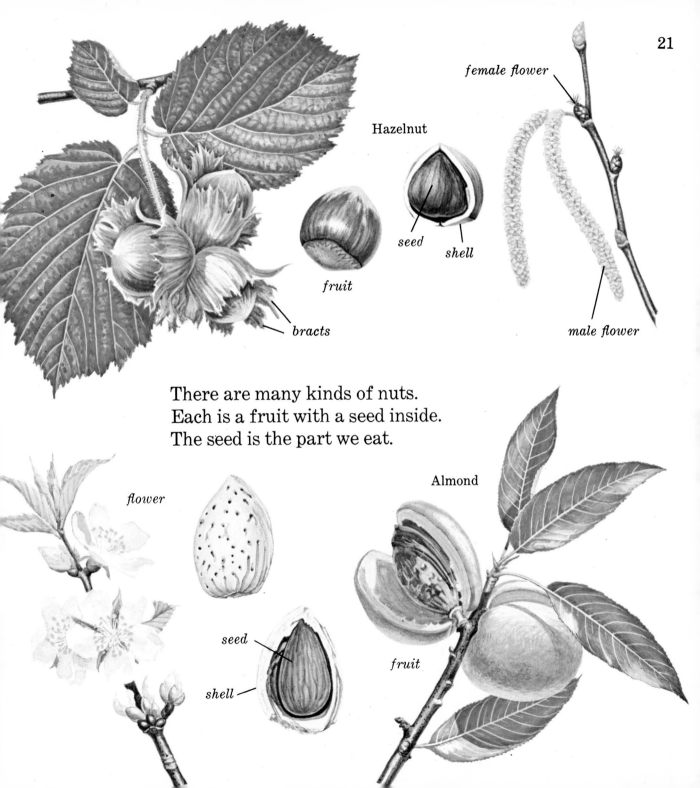

female flower

Hazelnut

seed

shell

fruit

male flower

bracts

There are many kinds of nuts.
Each is a fruit with a seed inside.
The seed is the part we eat.

flower

Almond

seed

shell

fruit

*one flower
with many ovaries*

A strawberry is a fruit.
A strawberry is a sweet
  juicy fruit with
  the fleshy part on the
  inside and many seeds
  on the outside.
A strawberry comes from
  a flower that has
  many ovaries.
Each ripened ovary
  develops a seed.

fruit

seeds

Blackberry

Blackberries and raspberries are fruits.
Each fruit comes from a single flower.
Each flower has many ovaries.
Each ripened ovary develops a seed.

seeds

Raspberry

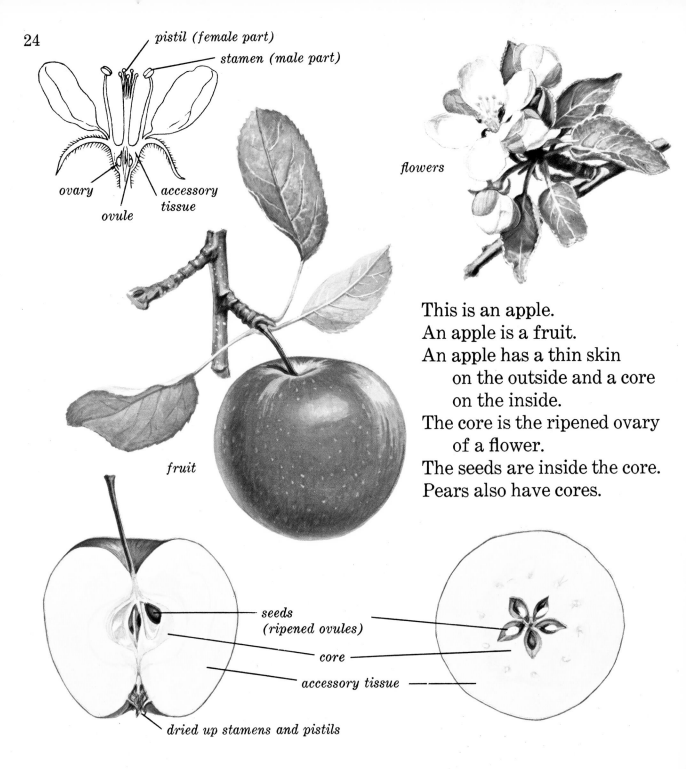

pistil (female part)

stamen (male part)

ovary

ovule

accessory
tissue

flowers

fruit

This is an apple.
An apple is a fruit.
An apple has a thin skin
    on the outside and a core
    on the inside.
The core is the ripened ovary
    of a flower.
The seeds are inside the core.
Pears also have cores.

seeds
(ripened ovules)

core

accessory tissue

dried up stamens and pistils

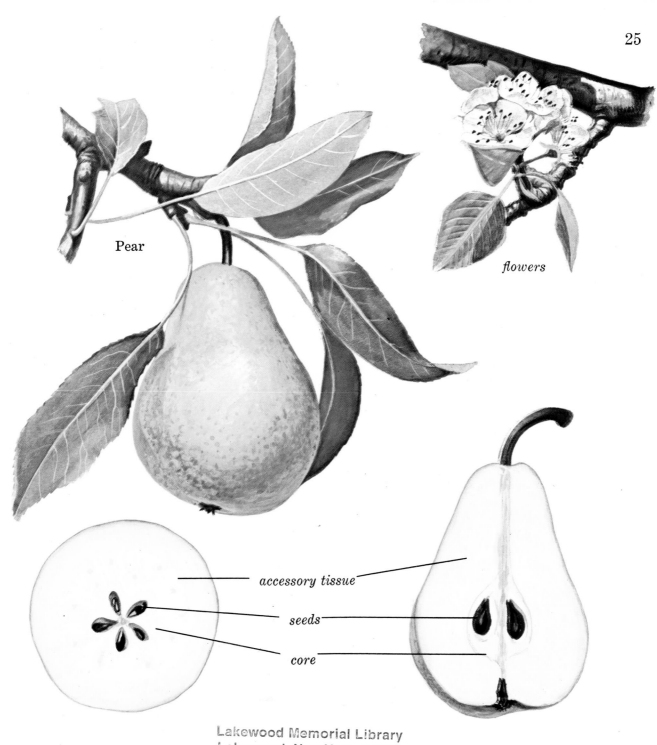

Pear

flowers

accessory tissue

seeds

core

26

Oat

Sunflower

Caraway

Apricot

Bean

Coconut

Acorn

Nutmeg   Milkweed   Chestnut

There are many kinds of fruits.
There are many shapes of fruits.
There are many sizes of fruits.
There are juicy fruits and dry fruits,
    soft fruits and hard fruits.
There are fruits with smooth skins,
    leathery skins, fuzzy skins, tough
    skins, thin skins and thick skins.
Some fruits have one seed, others
    have many seeds, and some have no seeds.
Some fruits are sweet; some fruits are not.
Some fruits may be eaten; some fruits may not.
There are many kinds of fruits.

But what is a fruit?

A fruit is the ripened ovary of a flower.
A fruit usually has seeds.
Seeds are the beginnings of new plants.

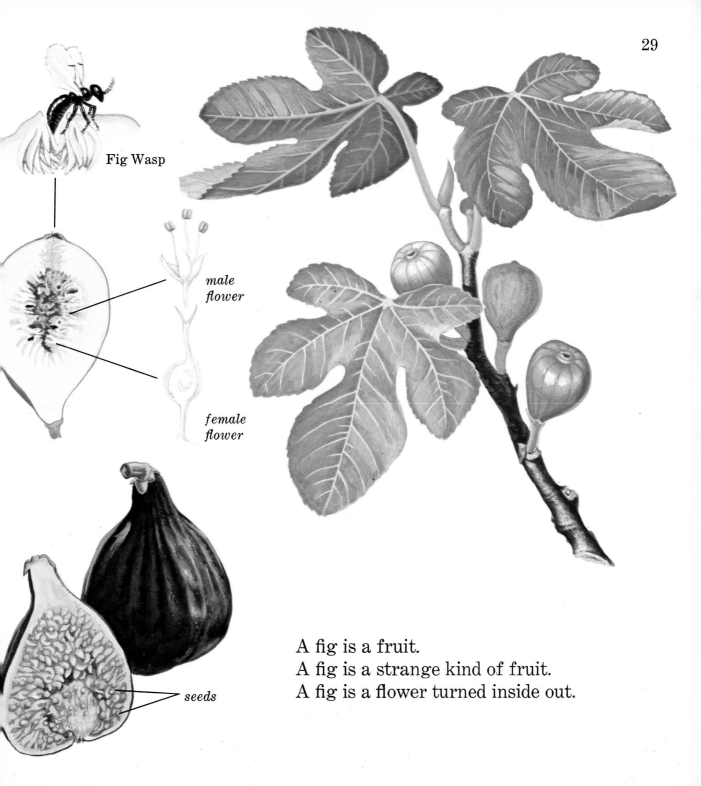

Fig Wasp

male
flower

female
flower

seeds

A fig is a fruit.
A fig is a strange kind of fruit.
A fig is a flower turned inside out.

WORD LIST

WORDS THAT NAME

apple	grain(s)	ovules	shell
banana	inside	part	sizes
beginnings	kinds	peach	skin
berries	legumes	pears	some
blackberries	many	peas	stalk
core(s)	nuts	plants	strawberry
corn	one(s)	pod(s)	tomato
each	orange	raspberries	vegetable
ear	others	rice	walnut
fig(s)	outside	rind	watermelon
flower(s)	ovaries	seed(s)	we
fruit(s)	ovary	shapes	wheat

WORDS THAT DESCRIBE

all	green	ripened	stony
citrus	hard	simple	sweet
dry	juicy	single	thick
fleshy	leathery	smooth	thin
flowering	many	soft	tough
fuzzy	new	some	wild

ACTION WORDS

are	comes	eaten	is
be	develop(s)	has	may
called	eat	have	turned

NOTE TO PARENTS AND TEACHERS

Children today are faced with a knowledge explosion unprecedented in recorded time. It is forcing parents, educators, and publishers to reexamine the kinds of books we place at their disposal. We must take shortcuts to expedite and expand their level of understanding. For that reason, this book, which is one of a series, has been designed as a beginner's introduction to concept development.

Botanically, a "fruit" is clearly distinguished from the common concept of its being only a soft, sweet, edible plant part. Fruits may vary in form, texture and structure and may be classified accordingly. This book introduces to children the notion of classification by using a representative sampling of different types of fruits, identifying each type illustrated by its common name. At the same time the differences among fruits are being displayed, the concept is developed that a fruit is the ripened ovary of a flower and usually contains the seeds of the next generation.

Flowering plants, about 250,000 species, include trees, vines, shrubs and herbaceous plants. The type of flower, fruit and seed is usually distinctive for each family.

This simple introduction to fruits may generate among young children an interest in knowing more about the role that flowers, fruits and seeds play in the continuity of life.

While there has been no attempt to restrict the vocabulary to conform to standard readability levels, there has been an attempt to repeat words often enough to develop word recognition, even among the very young. It is supposed that this book may be used with children who are, as yet, non-readers. It is the philosophy of the author that many children suffer from mental retardation engendered by an all too common malady—lack of exposure. For that reason, there has been a deliberate introduction of words not usually found in books for this age level, but only those words needed to convey the concepts of diversity and uniformity among living things. It is to be assumed that any word that is understood orally may be learned visually, especially if it is encountered often enough to make an indelible impression.

The word list found on pages 30-31 has been included for those of you who wish to help some child practice word recognition out of context. The words have been divided into three groups according to the way they have been used in the text. Not all words used have been listed. At no time is it suggested that the use of the word list be extended beyond the child's own interest in learning the words included. It is simply an optional memory exercise.